English words that come from Italian

umbrella   broccoli   studio

piano   opera

volcano   cameo   torso

Welcome to Italy

Meredith Costain   Paul Collins

This edition first published in 2002 in the United States of America by Chelsea House Publishers, a subsidiary of Haights Cross Communications

Chelsea House Publishers
1974 Sproul Road, Suite 400
Broomall, PA 19008–0914

The Chelsea House world wide web address is www.chelseahouse.com

Library of Congress Cataloging-in-Publication Data Applied for.
ISBN 0-7910-6550-2

First published in 2000 by
Macmillan Education Australia Pty Ltd
627 Chapel Street, South Yarra, Australia, 3141

Copyright © Meredith Costain and Paul Collins 2000

Edited by Miriana Dasovic
Text design by Goanna Graphics (Vic) Pty Ltd
Page layout by Goanna Graphics (Vic) Pty Ltd
Cover design by Goanna Graphics (Vic) Pty Ltd
Printed in Hong Kong

Acknowledgements
The author and the publisher are grateful to the following for permission to reproduce copyright material:

Cover photograph: Feeding pigeons in the Piazza della Signoria, Florence, © Blaine Harrington.

Auscape, p. 20 (top) © Jean-Paul Ferrero, p. 21 (top) © Ferrero-Labat, p. 21 (bottom) © Mark Hamblin-Oxford Scientific Films; Angela Berry, pp. 11 (bottom), 20 (bottom), 30; Angela Costain, pp. 10, 25 (top), 27 (bottom); Great Southern Stock, p. 14, p. 19 (bottom) © A Gregory; Blaine Harrington, pp. 5, 6, 7 (top), 8, 12, 13 (top & bottom), 18, 22, 23 (bottom), 24, 25 (bottom), 26, 27 (top), 28; Lonely Planet Images, p. 7 (bottom) © John Hay, pp. 11 (top) & 15 © Christopher Groenhout, pp. 19 (top), 23 (top) & 29 © Jon Davison; Sport. The Library, p. 9 (top) © Paolo Maldini-Coppo Campioni, p. 9 (bottom) © Claudio Chiappucci.

While every care has been taken to trace and acknowledge copyright the publishers tender their apologies for any accidental infringement where copyright has proved untraceable.

Contents

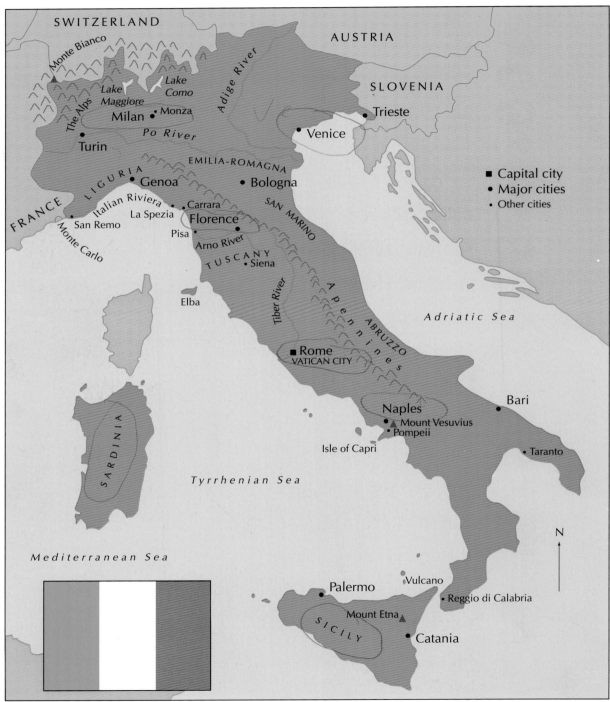

SWITZERLAND

AUSTRIA

Monte Bianco

Adige River

SLOVENIA

The Alps

Lake Maggiore

Lake Como

Milan • Monza

Trieste

Turin

Po River

Venice

EMILIA-ROMAGNA

LIGURIA

Genoa • Bologna

■ Capital city
• Major cities
• Other cities

Italian Riviera

Carrara

San Marino

FRANCE

San Remo

La Spezia

Florence

Monte Carlo

Pisa

Arno River

TUSCANY • Siena

Apennines

ABRUZZO

Adriatic Sea

Elba

Tiber River

Rome
VATICAN CITY

Naples

Bari

Mount Vesuvius
• Pompeii

SARDINIA

Isle of Capri

Taranto

Tyrrhenian Sea

Mediterranean Sea

N

Palermo

Vulcano

Reggio di Calabria

SICILY

Mount Etna

Catania

Welcome to Italy!

Ciao! My name is Cinzia. I come from Portofino, a fishing village near La Spezia in northern Italy. This area, which is very popular for holidays, is called the Riviera.

Italy is in southern Europe. It is shaped like a long, thin, high-heeled boot. The toe of the boot looks as if it is kicking the island of Sicily into the Mediterranean Sea! There are several other islands belonging to Italy, including Elba, Sardinia and the beautiful Isle of Capri.

Italy is divided into 20 regions and has two independent states, the Vatican City in Rome, and the Republic of San Marino. Our neighbors are France, Switzerland, Austria and Slovenia. Our flag has three vertical stripes in green, white and red.

Italy is famous for many things. Tourists come from all over the world to admire our paintings and sculptures, and to visit our churches. They also enjoy our weather, and, most of all, eat our food! Italians are also famous for being adventurous. Our famous explorers and navigators include Christopher Columbus, Amerigo Vespucci and Marco Polo.

Family life

Portofino is in Liguria, one of Italy's smallest regions. People say it is the most beautiful place on Earth! It has a tiny harbor filled with yachts, and a sandy beach. An old castle looks down on the village, and a lighthouse helps to guide boats at sea. The mountains along the coast are filled with wildflowers and olive groves. The mountain roads are often filled with sports cars on their way to Monte Carlo.

The houses in my village are painted in lots of different colors. Every summer, tourists come here to sit on the beach or in the cafés, or to shop in the smart boutiques. My mother works in a dress shop. My father works on the harbor, hiring out yachts to tourists.

My village has a lovely harbor, lined with cafés and shops. The land behind the houses is very steep. On Sundays, my family goes to our local church, San Giorgio.

I have a little sister, Antonella, and a brother, Ennio. Our grandmother, who lives with us, helps to look after Antonella when my parents are at work. Her brother, **Zio** Enrico, lives next-door. He spends most days fishing with his friends from the village. My other grandparents live in Florence. I love visiting them, because there are so many wonderful things to see there.

*Every year we visit my **nonna** and **nonno** in Florence. Ennio likes feeding the pigeons in the Piazza della Signoria.*

Zio Enrico enjoys fishing with his friends.

School

Italian children start school when they are six. Many children go to preschool first for a couple of years, to help them get ready for school. At the end of primary school, we move up to first level (junior) secondary school for three years. Then, if we want to go further, we move on to second level (senior) secondary school for another five years. We have exams at the end of every year.

There are two types of senior secondary schools. At the *liceo*, students do subjects such as science and languages. At the end of this course, they have very hard exams. If they pass these exams, they can go on to university.

At technical schools, students learn to work in agriculture or industry. Some of them train to be teachers.

I go to school six days a week. My school day starts at 8:30 a.m. and finishes at lunchtime. I study reading, maths, history, science, music, and art, my favorite subject.

These students are playing basketball at lunchtime.

Sports and leisure

Our national sport is soccer. We call it *calcio*. Every Sunday, people all over the country rush to their local stadium or flick on the TV set to watch a soccer match. Our soccer teams, Juventas, Inter Milan and AC Milan, are some of the best in the world. Fans at soccer matches get very excited if their team wins. They rush onto the field and rip the shirts off the winning players.

Soccer is the national sport of Italy.

In winter, Italian people go skiing in the Alps and Apennines. Summer sports include swimming, sailing, fishing, hiking and mountain-climbing. The Giro d'Italia bicycle race is held every spring. Cyclists crisscross the country for three weeks. Another famous race is the Mille Miglia, a 1,600-kilometer (995 mile) motor race held on the open road. The Grand Prix is held at Monza, near Milan.

In the evenings, many people dress up and head outside for the *passeggiata,* a quiet walk through the main square of their town. It is a great way to meet friends and find out what has been happening.

Cyclists begin the race from Milan to San Remo.

Italian culture

Italy is often called the 'Land of Art'. Our whole country is a treasure-trove of magnificent paintings, sculpture and architecture. Although we have over 700 art galleries and museums, you do not need to visit one to see great art. There are fountains in town squares, sculptures in streets and parks, and paintings in churches.

The **Renaissance** was a great period of thinking, learning, writing and creating works of art in Italy's history. It began in Italy around 1300 and spread through the rest of Europe before ending around 1600. During this time, Italy produced some of the greatest artists, sculptors, architects and music composers in history.

Leonardo da Vinci was one of Italy's greatest artists. He was also a **sculptor**, a scientist, an architect, an inventor and an engineer. His paintings include the mysterious *Mona Lisa*, and *The Last Supper*, showing Jesus with his 12 disciples. Leonardo's drawings included types of planes, tanks, cars and submarines. He made them up because they did not exist then!

This is a copy of the famous statue of David *in Florence. The original statue is only one of many great works by Michelangelo. In 1508, he began to paint the ceiling of the Sistine Chapel in Rome with scenes from the Bible. These wall paintings, called* **frescos***, were painted while he was lying on his back on a* **scaffold***. They took him four years to complete.*

Renaissance painters chose most of their subjects from the Bible or from myths. Botticelli, Raphael and Titian all created pictures with lifelike figures and beautiful color and detail.

The first great works of literature in the Italian language were written around 1300 by the poet and author Dante Alighieri. His best-known work is called *The Divine Comedy*. It is about an imaginary journey through Heaven and Hell. Italy has also produced many famous composers and musicians. Opera was invented by Italians in the 1600s and works by the composers Rossini, Verdi and Puccini are still performed around the world. Europe's most famous opera house is La Scala in Milan. The audience is often very noisy during a performance. They clap and shout 'bravo' if they like it, and boo if they do not!

*The Roman Forum was a city square in the center of Rome during the days of the **Roman Empire**. The Forum contained government buildings, temples, law courts, shops and open spaces where the people could gather.*

A billboard on the wall of La Scala advertises the operas that will be performed there.

Festivals and religion

Ninety-nine percent of Italians are Roman Catholic. Once people's lives were ruled by the Church, but these days religion is becoming less important. My grandmother and her sister are the only members of my family who go to Mass every Sunday. The rest of us go for special occasions, such as Easter, Christmas and weddings.

The Vatican City, in the middle of Rome, is the smallest independent country in the world.

Many Italians are superstitious. We believe some things that cannot be proved. Some people believe in witches and werewolves. In Naples, there is a bottle which people say contains the blood of a saint. Every year a big ceremony is held to see whether the dried blood turns back to liquid blood. If it does, Neapolitans believe they will have good luck in the next year.

The Pope is the leader of the Catholic Church. He lives in Vatican City, an area inside the city of Rome. The Vatican is only a tiny city. Fewer than 1,000 people live there, and it only takes 5 minutes to walk from one side to the other. People come from all over the world to stand in the square outside St. Peter's Basilica in the Vatican and be blessed by the Pope.

We have many different festivals where we get together with our friends and relatives. Some are religious, such as the Easter processions at Taranto, where hooded men carry religious statues around the town. Others celebrate the end of the harvest, or a historic event. Florence hosts an annual football match in memory of the Florentines who played football while the city was under attack in 1530.

The Palio is a colorful, dangerous horse race held each year in the town square in Siena. The people dress up in fifteenth-century clothing, wave flags and play drums and trumpets

Italian Festivals and Holidays

New Year's Day	January 1
Carnevale	February/March
Easter	March/April
Liberation Day	April 25
Festival of Snakes (Abruzzo)	June
Palio (Siena)	July/August
Assumption of the Virgin	August 15
Historical Regatta (Venice)	September
All Saints' Day	November 1
Christmas	December 25

*People dress up in costumes and masks for Carnevale, a festival that lasts for 10 days before the start of **Lent**.*

Food and shopping

Italians love food! Italy is the home of many delicious dishes: pizza, spaghetti, cassata and gelati. Each region or city has its own specialty. In Liguria, my region, where olives and basil grow, people make *pasta pesto*. Parmesan cheese and *prosciutto*, a type of ham, come from Emilia-Romagna. *Minestrone* (a bean and vegetable soup) comes from Milan, *spaghetti Bolognaise* from Bologna, and *risotto* made with rice and peas from Venice. Naples is famous for its pizza.

Pasta is our national dish. It is made from flour and water, and sometimes eggs. There are more than 500 different types and shapes of pasta. The Italian names for some of them mean angel's hair, butterflies, little tongues, little moustaches and car-door handles.

Breakfast is a quick, simple meal. We usually have bread with coffee or hot chocolate. Lunch is the main meal of the day. We start off with a pasta dish, then have meat and vegetables and a salad. Then we will have a fruit tart, or fresh fruit and cheese. We have only a light meal in the evenings.

Pasta, our national dish, comes in many different shapes.

Every town square in Italy has a market place, selling fresh fruit and vegetables, meat and cheese.

My mother and grandmother do the shopping at the markets and small specialty shops in the village. The shops close for a few hours at lunchtime, but then stay open until late in the evening. There is fresh fish every day because we live on the coast. The markets also sell fresh fruit and vegetables, meat, cheese, salami, nuts and pastries.

Make a pizza

Ask an adult to help you prepare this dish.

Pizza is eaten in towns all over Italy, but its true home is Naples. Chefs in Naples have to serve a two- to three-year apprenticeship in pizza-making! Classic Neapolitan pizzas include *pizza marinara* (made with seafood, oregano, tomato sauce and garlic) and *pizza Margherita* (made with tomato sauce, cheese and basil).

This recipe makes two pizzas.

You will need:

- 250 grams (1 cup) flour
- 1 teaspoon dried yeast
- 150 milliliters (1/2 cup) warm water
- 1/2 tablespoon olive oil
- tomato purée
- assorted toppings: grated cheese, diced ham, bacon strips, sliced salami, oregano, onion rings, anchovies, red or green peppers, shrimp, olives

What to do:

1. Sift the flour into a big bowl. Add the yeast.

2. Pour in the water and oil. Mix together until it forms a dough.

3. Take the dough out of the bowl and place it on a floured board or benchtop. Knead the dough until it is smooth and stretchy.

4. Cover the dough with a damp cloth. Leave it in a warm place to rise for 30 minutes.

5. Grease two round 25 cm (9 in) baking trays. Divide the dough in half. Press each half into a tray.

6. Spread the tomato purée on the dough. Cover the pizza with your favourite toppings.

7. Bake the pizzas for half an hour at 180°C (350°F).

Make a mask for a masquerade ball

Masks were first worn by characters such as Harlequin and Punchinello in Italian plays of the 1300s. In later times, guests at balls and parties wore masks that covered their eyes so that they could take on a new personality for the evening. The balls were fun because people could never be sure who they were dancing with!

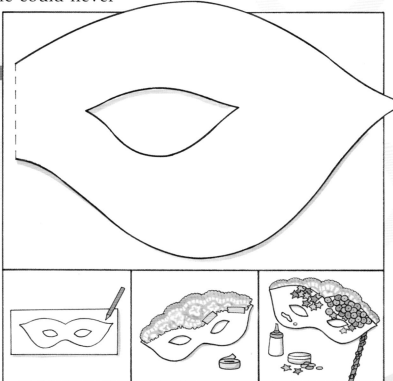

What you need:

- white paper
- posterboard or cardboard
- a paper doily
- sticky tape
- ruler
- pencil
- scissors
- a thin stick or cane
- sequins and small beads
- stringed sequins
- strong glue
- brush

What to do:

1   First make a paper pattern for the mask. Fold the white paper in half. Copy the large outline of the mask on this page, making it to the size shown.

2   Place the opened-out mask pattern on the cardboard. Draw around the shape, then cut it out, including the eye-holes.

3   Cut the frilly edge from a paper doily. Tape it across the top of the back of the mask. Cover the front of the mask with a thin layer of strong glue. Stick on layers of sequins and beads until the whole mask is covered.

4   Put dots of glue along a string of sequins and wind it around the stick. Tape the stick to one side of the back of the mask.

Hold the mask in front of your face and have fun looking mysterious!

Landscape and climate

Italy has several different regions, each with its own distinctive landscape and climate. Some of these regions are separated by natural boundaries, such as mountains or the sea.

Three-quarters of Italy is covered by mountains, and the rest by **plains**. The snowy Alps run across the north of the country. The tallest peak in Europe, Monte Bianco, is found here, on the border with France. It is known as 'white mountain' because it is covered in snow all year round. There are beautiful lakes, such as Lake Como and Lake Maggiore, in the foothills of the Alps. The Po Valley, at the western end of the Alps, has many rivers and rich soil. The Alps have long, harsh winters with lots of snow.

The long 'leg' part of Italy is a **peninsula**. A mountain range called the Apennines runs down the center of the country like a giant backbone. The climate in the low coastal areas of the peninsula is warm and pleasant, even in winter. The further south you go, the warmer and drier the weather becomes. The land in the south is less **fertile** than in the north.

*Lake Como, in the foothills of the Alps, is a popular holiday resort. It was formed long ago by a **glacier** carving out the valley.*

The Italian Riviera stretches from the French border to La Spezia. Behind the deep blue bays are high wooded mountains. The towns and villages are built on steep slopes. The islands of Sicily and Sardinia have long, hot, dry summers and mild winters. Vulcano, an island near the north coast of Sicily, is a **dormant** volcano, surrounded by boiling seas fed by hot springs.

Average temperatures

	January	June
Milan	1°C/34°F	24°C/75°F
Venice	3°C/37°F	24°C/75°F
Palermo	10°C/50°F	24°C/75°F

Tuscany, a large region in the central north, has rolling hills and a sunny climate.

Wildflowers grow in the north of Italy.

Plants and animals

Because people have farmed the land in Italy for centuries, there is little of the original forests left. **Evergreen** trees such as beeches, Norway spruce and other **conifers** grow in the Alpine regions. On lower ground there are **deciduous** trees such as oak, chestnut and poplar. Cypress and olive trees grow in the northern lake district. Almond and citrus trees grow naturally in the warmer climate of the south.

Wildcats can still be found in the Apennines.

Olive trees grow among grapevines and maize in Urbania, in northeastern Italy.

When the forests were cleared, many of the animals living there lost their homes and died out. But a few kinds of wild animals can still be found living in the mountain regions. Wild bears, badgers and wildcats live in the Apennines, and deer, wild goats and ibex live in the Alps.

Wolves can be found in the south of Italy, and wild boars and a type of wild sheep called mouflons are found on the island of Sardinia. The skies of Italy are home to falcons, hawks and golden eagles, and the Mediterranean is full of many types of fish. These include sardines, squid, tuna, shark and swordfish.

Ibex, a type of antelope, make their home in the Alps.

Badgers live in wooded areas.

Cities and landmarks

About three-quarters of Italians live in cities. There is not much space for houses in the cities, so most people live in apartment blocks. Rome, our capital, was built on seven hills. According to legend, it was built around 700 BC by Romulus and Remus, twins who were reared by a she-wolf when their uncle threw them into the River Tiber. Rome today is a mix of old buildings, squares and temples left over from the days of the Roman Empire, and modern, noisy streets lined with churches, grand hotels and pavement cafés.

*The Colosseum, in Rome, was a huge sports arena, seating 50,000 people. People came to watch **gladiators** fight with each other, or with wild animals, to the death. In one day in AD 80, there were 5,000 lions and elephants killed.*

Venice is a series of islands, canals and bridges, built on a **lagoon**. People get around by either steamboat, called *vaporetto*, or on motorboats called *motoscafi*. Only tourists travel by gondola these days. The **gondoliers** punt the boats by hand, and often sing as they work. Tourists flock to Venice every year to see its beautiful squares, called piazzas, and its palaces and churches.

Florence, on the banks of the River Arno, has many churches and palaces brimming with paintings and sculptures. People flock to the northern city of Milan for its fashion, restaurants, art galleries and opera. They also visit its Renaissance castle and its cathedral, the fourth-largest in the world.

The Leaning Tower of Pisa was built 800 years ago. Soon after it was finished, the foundations began to sink. Every year it leans a tiny bit further to one side. Engineers are trying to find ways to stop it from falling over.

Taking a trip on a gondola is the best way to see the fine palaces that line the Grand Canal.

Industry and agriculture

Before World War 2, Italy was mainly a farming country. Today, it has thousands of modern factories, making many different kinds of goods. Italy is now one of the five most **industrialized** countries in the world.

Most industry in Italy is found in the triangle formed by the cities of Genoa, Turin and Milan. Many people have moved from the poorer areas of the south to find work in factories which process iron, steel, chemicals and textiles. Turin is the home of car manufacturing, which is one of Italy's biggest employers and largest exporters. Cars made here include Fiat, Lancia, Lamborghini, Alfa Romeo and Ferrari.

The marble produced at Carrara, in the north, is world-famous. Michelangelo used marble from this region for his sculptures.

Italy has now passed France as the world leader in fashion and design. Fashion shows in Milan, Rome and Florence are attended by buyers from all over the world, eager to get their hands on the latest designs by the fashion houses of Valentino, Fendi and Gucci.

The letters FIAT stand for

F   Fabbrica (factory)

I   Italiana (Italian)

A   Automobilistica (of automobiles)

T   Torino (at Turin)

Other well-known Italian products include electrical goods such as typewriters, sewing machines, refrigerators and washing machines, and processed food such as cheese, sausages and olive oil. Italy is also a world leader in the fields of electronics, optics, telecommunications, aeronautics and robotics.

Many people, like this gondolier in Venice, work in the tourist industry.

Most farms in Italy are quite small, and are usually worked by the owners and their families. Nearly half the farms grow grapes for wine. Other farmers grow cereal crops such as wheat and maize. Rice is grown in the fertile areas around the Po Valley. Farmers in the south grow vegetables, citrus fruits and olives. Italy makes the most olive oil and wine in the world!

Dairy farms are found throughout the country, but mainly in Emilia-Romagna, which is famous for its parmesan cheese. Farmers also raise pigs, cattle, sheep, goats, horses and poultry.

These farmers are cutting hay in the Alps.

Transportation

The hills and mountains of Italy have always made it difficult for people to get around. Two thousand years ago, the Romans built a system of roads across the country to help people move from town to town. Some of these roads are still used today.

Cars are the main form of transportation in Italy. Most families have at least one car, and they enjoy driving. Our car is a Fiat. The roads here are very good. Over the past 30 years, the government has spent huge amounts of money building superhighways, called **autostrade**. There are nearly 6,000 kilometers (3,728 miles) of *autostrade,* making it the third-largest road network in the world. The speed limit on these highways is 130 kilometers (81 miles) per hour, and people pay tolls to use them. The most famous route is *Autostrada del Sole,* which runs the length of Italy, from Milan in the north to Reggio di Calabria.

Motorscooters are as common as cars on the streets of Florence. The Vespa, invented in 1944, was the world's first motorscooter.

Train travel in Italy is fast and cheap. We have different types of trains, ranging from the long-distance *espresso* and *rapido* trains, to the local *accellerato*. Extremely fast trains, like the TEE, link Italy with northern Europe.

Italy has many ports along its long coastline, used by both passenger and cargo ships. Our main ports are Genoa, Trieste, Venice, Naples and La Spezia. Ferries and hydrofoils link the islands with the mainland. People also use ferries to get around on the lakes in the north.

Trams are an easy way to get around the streets of Milan.

Many people rely on boats to deliver the mail in Venice.

History and government

In ancient times, many different groups of people lived in Italy. The first settlers arrived from Asia over 30,000 years ago. The Etruscans arrived in about 1200 BC, followed by the Greeks, the Phoenicians, the Normans and the Gauls.

In about 754 BC, a group known as the Romans founded their capital city on the banks of the River Tiber. One hundred and fifty years later they defeated the Etruscans, who until then had dominated central Italy. The first Roman Republic was formed, which was ruled by the people rather than a king.

The Romans were well-organized and hard-working, with well-equipped armies. By 272 BC, the Romans controlled the whole of the Italian mainland. Four hundred years later, they ruled most of the known world, from Britain to Africa. They built roads, bridges and **aqueducts** across their empire, and magnificent structures such as the Colosseum and the Roman Forum in the center of Rome.

Eventually, around AD 200, the Roman Empire began to crumble. The land fell to barbarians, a Latin word meaning 'foreigners'. They were the Visigoths from Western Russia, and the Vandals from Hungary.

Ancient ruins, such as Emperor Hadrian's Villa near Tivoli, remind people of the time when Rome ruled the world.

By 1200, most of Italy was divided into tiny city-states, each based on a main city such as Florence, Venice or Milan. Run by rich and powerful families, each city-state had its own customs and language. These states were finally united into a single country in 1870.

In AD 79 Mount Vesuvius erupted, covering in ash the Roman city of Pompeii and the 20,000 people who lived there. In the 1800s, archaeologists began discovering bodies preserved in the ruins.

Italy today

Italy has been a democratic **republic** since 1946. Since then, our country has been very unstable politically. Forty-nine separate governments were formed between 1946 and 1990.

The Italian Parliament has two houses, the Chamber of Deputies and the Senate, with members elected by popular vote. A president is elected by Parliament to be head of the republic. However, the prime minister takes care of most of the day-to-day running of the country.

Fact file

Official name *Repubblica Italiana* (Republic of Italy)		**Population** 57,000,000	**Land area** 301,225 square kilometers (117,477 square miles)
Government republic	**Languages** Italian (each region has its own dialect)		**Religion** Christianity (Roman Catholic)
Currency Lira (£)		**Capital city** Rome	**Major cities** Milan, Naples, Turin, Genoa, Palermo, Florence, Bologna, Catania, Bari, Venice, Trieste
		Climate mild Mediterranean, with hot summers and cold northern winters	
Major rivers Po, Arno, Tiber, Adige			**Highest mountain** Monte Bianco 4,807 meters (15,770 feet)
Main farm products wheat, rice, grapes, olives, citrus fruits, cattle, sheep, goats, pigs	**Main industries** textiles, clothing, leather goods, cars, electrical goods, chemicals, marble, iron, steel, food processing, shoes		**Natural resources** fish, natural gas, marble, mercury, sulfur

Glossary

aqueduct	a structure which carries water across a valley or over a river
autostrade	superhighways, with a speed limit of 130 km (81 mi) per hour
conifers	trees with needle-like leaves
deciduous	plants and trees that lose their leaves in winter
dormant	sleeping, inactive
evergreen	plants and trees that do not lose their leaves in winter
fertile	rich, able to produce large amounts of crops
fresco	a painting done on fresh plaster, so that the paint colors are absorbed
glacier	a mass of ice that moves very slowly
gladiator	a slave who fought with weapons in public to entertain people
gondolier	a person who works on a boat called a gondola
industrialized	a country which uses machinery in farming and making products
lagoon	an area of shallow water
Lent	a time of prayer and fasting leading up to Easter
liceo	academic secondary school
nonna	grandmother
nonno	grandfather
peninsula	a piece of land, often narrow, that juts out from the mainland
plains	a large area of flat land
Renaissance	a period of great artistic, scientific and literary achievement that began in Italy around 1300
republic	a state in which the head of government is elected by the people
Roman Empire	countries ruled by Rome from 27 BC to AD 284
scaffold	a raised platform that holds workers
sculptor	an artist who carves figures from stone or wood
zio	uncle

Index